W9-DFD-966

ideals EASTER

Long days, beneath the cold of winter skies,
When beauty fades but promise never dies,
The Earth, with calm and tender brooding care,
Has nurtured life, secure within her lair.
In early spring, the sun with radiant charm,
Draws living buds, still shy of worldly harm,
To lead them gently through the April rain
In Easter garments, bright with rainbow stain.

Leila Bishopp Martin

ISBN 0-8249-1041-9

Publisher, Patricia A. Pingry
Editor/Ideals, Ramona Richards
Art Director, Jennifer Rundberg
Staff Artist, David Lenz
Permissions, Kathleen Gilbert
Copy Editor, Susan DuBois

IDEALS—Vol. 43, No. 2 March MCMLXXXVI IDEALS (ISSN 0019-137X) is published eight times a year,
February, March, May, June, August, September, November, December
by IDEALS PUBLISHING CORPORATION, Nelson Place at Elm Hill Pike, Nashville, Tenn. 37214
Second class postage paid at Nashville, Tennessee, and additional mailing offices.
Copyright © MCMLXXXVI by IDEALS PUBLISHING CORPORATION.
POSTMASTER: Send address changes to Ideals, Post Office Box 148000, Nashville, Tenn. 37214
All rights reserved. Title IDEALS registered U.S. Patent Office.
Published simultaneously in Canada.

SINGLE ISSUE—$3.50
ONE-YEAR SUBSCRIPTION—eight consecutive issues as published—$15.95
TWO-YEAR SUBSCRIPTION—sixteen consecutive issues as published—$27.95
Outside U.S.A., add $4.00 per subscription year for postage and handling.

The cover and entire contents of IDEALS are fully protected by copyright and must
not be reproduced in any manner whatsoever. Printed and bound in U.S.A.
by The Banta Co., Menasha, Wisconsin.

Front and back covers by Gene Ahrens

Inside front and back covers by Jeff Wiles/Peregrine Photo

Easter

Easter is a time for joy,
A time when all the earth is new;
A season when our thoughts reach out
To those whose friendships have been true.

Easter is a time for faith
That peace will someday rule the earth;
A faith that is well fortified,
As barren lands portray rebirth.

Easter is a time for praise,
Since everything on earth gives hope
That resurrection can be ours
Beyond this earthly lifetime scope.

Beatrice Branch

Looking for Spring

What do you look for, while searching for spring?
A small budding crocus, a bird on the wing,
Or maybe a blue sky, so wondrous and gay
A bit of green grass as you travel your way.

What do you look for when April is due?
The last winter snowflake before March is through,
A kite overhead for a youngster's delight
Or maybe the joy of a bright star-filled night.

Spring brings us wonders like none we have known
A brand new beginning to have for our own,
So much that holds beauty in each shining dawn
The warmth of the sunshine tells winter is gone.

What do you look for, there's so much to find,
A moment of peace for a bright hopeful mind,
A faith or a courage, a heart filled with mirth
When you look for springtime, do look for rebirth.

Garnett Ann Schultz

It's Almost Spring, Lord

It's almost spring, Lord.
Smudged snowdrifts cower
   beside thawing highways.
An adventurous crocus
   pokes through ground
   still cold from February frost.

It's almost Easter.
And I think of you, Lord,
   in your innocence
         humiliation
         sacrifice.

It is time
   for the eternal paradox
   for the blossoming and greening
      of stark brown branches
   for the renewing
      of life long dormant.

I think of the
   divine paradox of
     my life
   through
     your death.

And I am humbled
     saddened
thankful for
   springtime
   a crocus
and you.

Mary Lou Carney

Little Crocus

Little Crocus, poking through,
Would I were as brave as you.
You're the scout the tulips send
To report the winter's end.
Hyacinth and Daffodil
Fear the earth above is chill.
Underground the bulblets cheer
When they hear you volunteer,
You, who seem to have no fear.

Breaking ground with grass-like leaves,
You the snowy earth receives,
Smiling at your fragile form,
Smiling 'til itself is warm. . .
Warm enough to open up
Your wee funnel-fashioned cup.
"All is well" you notify
Those for whom you are the spy.
Then they, too, push toward the sky.

Little Crocus, I can see
Size of courage isn't wee
Just because a plant is small.
You're the bravest of them all.
They in all the hues God made
Soon will venture on parade,
But I wonder what they'd do
Without you to lead them through.
Would I were as brave as you!

Margaret Rorke

Country Chronicle

Coming as it does in the spring, I like to think of Easter as the sunrise of the year, the resurrection. It is the beginning of bird songs and garden blooms, the bud and leaf, the warming earth and planting time, the longer days of sunlight and clear blue skies. It is a renewal and rebirth, the inception of a recurring cycle in the seasons. There is no finality; one leads to another with positive certainty.

All about us are the colors of the floral Easter parade, the blooms of tulips and lilies, jonquils and daffodils, hyacinths and violets. The greening grass is like a bright new carpet spread upon the hills by the rains and the rays of a glowing sun.

The bogs and marshlands are warm with renewed and flowing life. The catkins of pussy willows display their finery while the shrill piping notes of the peepers fill the late afternoon and evening hours with an incessant din of musical bells. Brooks and streams are open; their liquid waters sing in splashing overtones.

There are bird songs from robins, redwings, song sparrows, white-throats and white-crowns. The piercing call of the killdeer comes from the wild pasture beyond the barns.

One of the most moving and inspiring

bird songs is the liquid warble of the bluebird, so rich and tender it seems to thaw the sharpness of these early morning hours. Like the sun drawing the frost from the ground and urging the sap to rise in the maple, it warms the heart of a man who has long been a part of the land.

Several years ago, a white bluebird brought an Easter surprise when it came to our backyard. It was sheer white, and its eyes were as pink as some of the hues that come over the eastern horizon at dawn. We saw the albino for several days; then it was gone. We assumed it joined in the migration to northern nesting grounds.

It was Thoreau, I believe, who so appropriately described the bluebird as "carrying the sky on its back." I wonder what words the naturalist would have used to describe our unusual Easter visitor, "floating" through the springtime rivers of air like a white feather in a gentle wind. He may well have thought of it as a bluebird whose sky-blue plumage had been dusted by an Easter snow.

The dawn of a new spring and the glory of the sunrise are an enduring assurance of the resurrection and everlasting life.

Lansing Christman

Readers' Reflections

Sing Me a Song

Sing me a song of the olden days,
The days now gone in a happy haze.
So nice to remember, so hard to believe
They could have happened beyond reprieve.

Sing me a song of quiet nights
When the world is turning out the lights,
When the workday is ended and quiet sublime,
And our daily reward is the gift of time.

Sing me a song of the world at peace,
No worry that wars would never cease,
No worry that nations would plot conquest
And power the object of all behest.

Sing me a song of a Sunday, fair
When all went to church and met everyone there.
A small part of day for quiet and prayer
To get prepared for the next week's fare.

Sing me a song!!

Thomas T. McDonald
Peterborough, New Hampshire

Herald of Springtime

The sun is dimly shining,
It's a cold and blustery day.
You may not believe it,
But spring is on its way.

It's not the swelling budlets
On the shadowy branches of trees,
Nor the squirrels I watch leaping,
Nor the slowly waking bees.

It's not the trustful grass
A bit greener day by day,
Nor the small brave daffodils
Looking bright and gay.

It's not just the robin's
Or chickadee's call so clear.
It's the garden catalogs coming,
Telling me that spring is near.

They say that I should get busy
And plan my garden soon,
For Nature suddenly will be shouting,
"Spring's symphony is now in tune."

Louise Taylor Tucker
Erie, Pennsylvania

Photo Overleaf
DANDELIONS
Gene Ahrens

Songbird Choir

There's a serenade of songbirds
That awakens my yard each day,
Just when the sun is on the rise,
And the rabbits come out to play.

The cardinal calls his "Pretty Girl,"
But the chickadee seems to reply.
And the wren sings such a vibrant song
For such a little guy.

There are sparrows on the clothesline,
And robins perched in the trees.
They're all singing songs together
With different melodies.

The bluejay and the thrush join in,
Each with their own special song,
To serenade the passing deer
That just happened along.

They're such a faithful little group,
Cheerful in sun or shower,
And I'm glad they picked my backyard
'Cause I love my songbird choir.

Isabell Niland
Westernport, Maryland

Yellow Daffodils

Blue skies tell me that spring is here
With freshest air from distant hills;
White blossoms on fruit trees appear
And I see yellow daffodils.

When snow is gone and ground is bare
And birds begin their flute-like trills,
Bright flowers pop up everywhere
The brightest—yellow daffodils.

I love to hear a robin sing
And watch it drink where water spills,
I love the beauty springtime brings—
My choice is yellow daffodils.

Edith Baglo
Duncan, British Columbia

Editor's Note: Readers are invited to submit poetry, short anecdotes, and humorous reflections on life for possible publication in future *Ideals* issues. Please send copies only; manuscripts will not be returned. Writers will receive $10 for each published submission. Send materials to "Readers' Reflections," Ideals Publishing Corporation, Nelson Place at Elm Hill Pike, Nashville, Tennessee 37214.

The Lamb

Little Lamb, who made thee?
Dost thou know who made thee;
Gave thee life and bid thee feed
By the stream and o'er the mead;
Gave thee clothing of delight,
Softest clothing, woolly, bright;
Gave thee such a tender voice
Making all the vales rejoice?
Little Lamb, who made thee?
Dost thou know who made thee?

Little Lamb, I'll tell thee,
Little Lamb, I'll tell thee;
He is called by thy name,
For He calls Himself a Lamb.
He is meek and He is mild;
He became a little child.
I a child and thou a lamb,
We are called by His name.
Little Lamb, God bless thee.
Little Lamb, God bless thee.

William Blake

When I Was Six

When I was only six, my dear,
And orchards were in bloom,
I used to look for Easter eggs
In every place and room.

When I was only six, my dear,
I searched from east to west
Until I found some Easter eggs
Hidden in a rabbit's nest.

The rabbit still lingered there,
And it had left for me
Some bright and shining colored eggs
Beneath a snow-white tree.

Now that I am no longer six
I journey back each spring
To find the rabbit's cozy nest
And hear a robin sing.

And there again I find the eggs
Of red and green and blue,
And once again I keep the faith
of Easter time—don't you?

Frances Bowles

Photo Opposite
EASTER GREETINGS
Three Lions

Easter Happiness

Easter's a happy time
   of the year
With new clothes
   and happy faces,
And the chance to visit
   Grandma's house
Or other friendly places.

A trip to the country
   for some of us
And we leave right
   after church,
To hide the many
   colored eggs
Then help the children search.

To see them run
   and wander about
And no place do
   they overlook,
Their squeals of excitement
   and words of joy
Are enough to fill a book.

Yes, Easter is fun
   for all of us
As anyone will say—
How much they enjoy
   the happiness found
In every Easter Day.

LaVonne Carmincke

Coloring Eggs

In the country long ago
Eggs were colored touch-and-go;
We didn't have a color kit
But each egg had a gay outfit.

Mom saved scraps that faded red
Eggs were wrapped and tied with thread,
I loved the ones in calico
They were special touch-and-go.

We gathered grass to make them green
These in kit were never seen;
An artist with the finest brush
Could never paint a green so lush.

When they'd boiled and cooled enough
We took off the dressing stuff;
Oh, what colors and what glow
We had made with touch-and-go!

Laurie Dawson

Photo Overleaf
COLORING EGGS
H. Armstrong Roberts

How the Egg Got into Easter

Many people do not know that Easter originated as a celebration to honor the Teutonic goddess of spring, Eostre, who returned each year to bring spring back to the people after the long gloomy months of winter. As a result, many of the customs we observe at Easter time are not based on religious traditions but are carried down from medieval and ancient times by legends and folklore.

The Easter egg remains one of the most widely observed symbols of Easter. Do you know when the Easter egg made its first appearance, and how or why?

The tradition of hiding Easter eggs to be discovered Easter morning started long ago when a poor mother in Germany dyed some hard-boiled eggs as gifts for her children during a famine. She built a little nest in the yard as a hiding place and tucked the eggs inside. The next morning when the children discovered the nest, a little rabbit jumped out of it and hopped away. The notion that the bunny had laid the eggs was such a charming idea that the Easter Bunny hopped its way from Germany over to France and Belgium and, finally, to the United States.

Little children in olden times made nests of straw and stick on Easter Eve and waited for the Easter Bunny to fill them with eggs much as youngsters today hang their stockings for Santa Claus to fill them with small presents.

During the Middle Ages, colored eggs were used as gifts in Egypt and Persia. Servants were given the eggs by their masters as rewards for being loyal and dutiful. After the

Crusades, this custom spread into Europe. According to one legend, King Edward I of England (who ruled from 1272 to 1307) once ordered 450 eggs to be boiled, colored and presented to his servants on Easter morning as gifts for their faithfulness.

One reason why eggs were popular at Easter was because the Christians who observed the Lenten season were not supposed to include meat or eggs in their diet. During the 40-day period between Ash Wednesday and Easter, the eggs that were laid by ducks, geese and chickens accumulated. To keep them from spoiling, they were stored in nests of sticks and stones in cool places. They were brought out to be hard-boiled and colored for decorations and gifts, or were eaten as a special treat on Easter Sunday.

Eggs were also used for contests. Children chased hard-boiled eggs down a hill or slope. The egg that reached the bottom without cracking was called the "victory egg," and the child who found it was given the grand prize of 101 hard-boiled eggs.

When colored eggs were first used in Italy, they were blessed by a priest, then arranged as colorful centerpieces for the dining room table on Easter Sunday. In some affluent homes, as many as 200 gaily-colored eggs were displayed in the center of the table.

Colored eggs were also carried for greetings. In Greece and Romania it was fashionable to carry red eggs which were used to greet friends met on the street or in the home. Instead of shaking hands or kissing cheeks, they tapped their red eggs together to say hello.

What better way to greet the coming of spring than to wish for good luck and happiness for yourself, your family, and your friends? You can do this by putting the egg into your Easter traditions, and make it more interesting by knowing how and when the egg got into Easter.

Vivian Buchan

Easter Morning

What a lovely Easter morning—
A smile on every face;
Children eager and waiting
To start the annual race.

Colored eggs are hidden
And chocolate bunnies too;
See the lovely colors
Of purple, orange, and blue.

A marshmallow chick of yellow
Peeks out from beneath a stump;
And a tiny chocolate rabbit
Peers around a grassy clump.

Beautiful woven baskets
Await sweet sugary fill,
As the blazing sun comes up
O'er the emerald grassy hill.

Ruth H. Underhill

Easter Bunny Lesson

I met the Easter Bunny
And he told this tale to me,
He said "I'm very busy
As you can plainly see.

"I go to visit children
At this time of the year,
I see their smiling faces
Whenever I appear.

"I leave them pretty baskets
Of every shape and size,
With eggs of dainty colors
To add to their surprise.

"How can I then be gloomy
While making others gay?"
Thus said the Easter Bunny
As he hopped upon his way.

Hilda Butler Farr

Funny Bunny

Over the grass he comes skippety-hop,
And it's almost certain he'll never stop
Till he reaches the house where Vicki lives
And delivers the basket that he gives
At Easter, to good little girls and boys,
Brimming over with candy eggs and toys.

With his fur so white and his eyes so pink
This busy bunny who's quick as a wink,
Wears a most becoming jacket of green
And the cutest bow-tie you've ever seen.

Just open your window the night before
And he'll hop right through to your bedroom floor;
Then nervously twitching whiskers funny,
Hides the eggs and leaves—this Easter Bunny.

Violet V. Moore

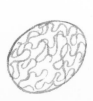

Easter Promise

It sometimes seems that wintertime
Will last forevermore,
And snow and sleet and biting winds
Are all life holds in store.

But suddenly a miracle
Takes place before our eyes...
The grass turns green and tulips bloom
Beneath bright springtime skies.

Thus is God's Easter pledge fulfilled
With every year that goes—
That life will spring from seeming death
As Christ the Savior rose.

Virginia Blanck Moore

Signs of Spring

When the mayapples flower
And the mushrooms are up,
When the violets dance beside
The yellow buttercups.

When the merry sunshine faces
Of the dandelions show,
When down in the garden
The peas start to grow.

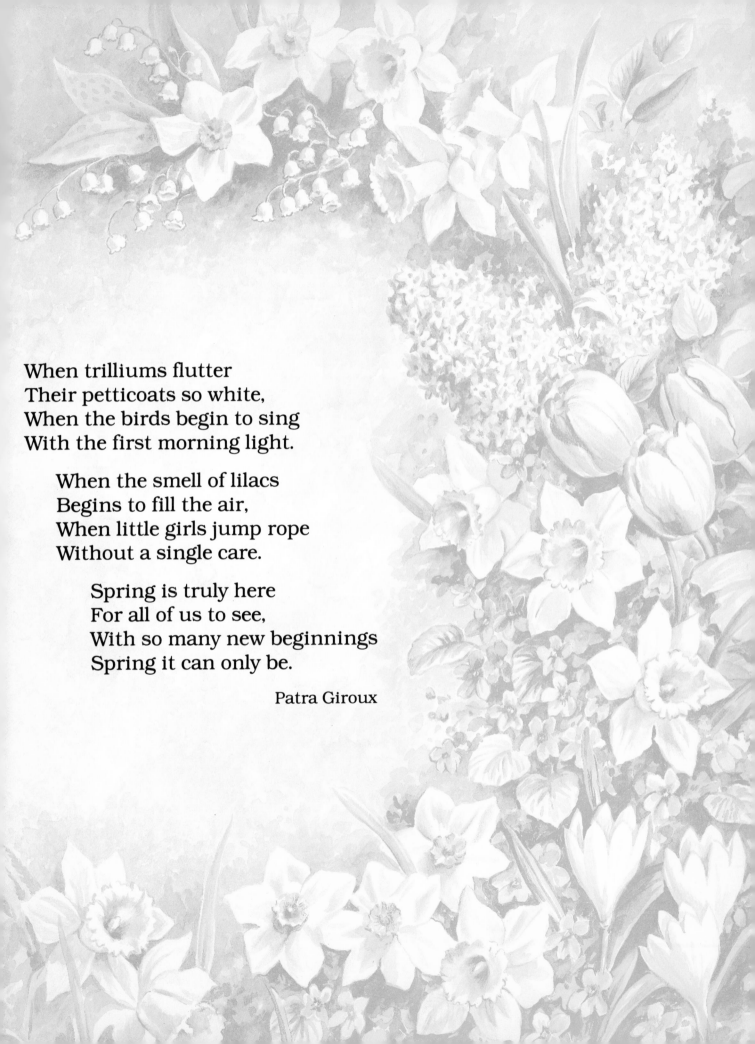

When trilliums flutter
Their petticoats so white,
When the birds begin to sing
With the first morning light.

When the smell of lilacs
Begins to fill the air,
When little girls jump rope
Without a single care.

Spring is truly here
For all of us to see,
With so many new beginnings
Spring it can only be.

Patra Giroux

Cenci
(Fried Italian Pastries)

Makes 20 Cannoli
20 Rectangles
36 Knots

3 cups flour
2 eggs, lightly beaten
3 tablespoons oil
2 tablespoons rum
2 to 3 tablespoons cold water
½ cup sugar
1 pound vegetable shortening
½ cup confectioners' sugar

Place the flour in a large bowl; form a well in the center. Place eggs, oil, rum, 2 tablespoons water, and sugar in well; stir ingredients together with a fork, working outward little by little to absorb all of the flour. Add remaining water if mixture is dry. Knead dough until very smooth and elastic. Wrap in plastic; set aside for 30 minutes. Roll dough out into a wide sheet ⅛-inch thick; cut into desired shapes. Heat shortening to 350⁰ in a deep saucepan. Fry the pastries a few at a time for 2 minutes or until golden brown on both sides. Drain on paper towels. Cool; sprinkle generously with confectioners' sugar.

Variations:

Rectangles

Cut the dough into 3 x 5-inch rectangles. Make three slits down the center of each rectangle, stopping ½-inch from each end.

Knots

Cut the dough into 10 x ½-inch strips; tie into a loose knot.

Cannoli

Cut the dough into 4 x 4-inch squares. Wrap the squares of dough around metal cannoli forms; pinch edges to form a tight seal. After pastries have cooled slightly, remove the cannoli form; fill each pastry with Cheese Filling. Dip ends in grated chocolate.

Cheese Filling

2 cups ricotta cheese
1¼ cups confectioners' sugar
1 cup heavy cream, whipped
¼ cup grated chocolate
½ cup chopped, candied citron
    Grated chocolate

Combine cheese and sugar; beat until smooth. Mix in all remaining ingredients except chocolate for dipping.

Remembering Easter

The textures were straw and dotted Swiss; the smells hyacinth and cellophane; the colors yellow and lavender.

The season was spring. The celebration was Easter.

Easter was always warm (or if it wasn't warm, I have chosen not to remember). The new grass of the lawn was showing green, not in a tidy blanket of uniform length, but in scattered tufts of unruly hair on a balding, brown head. The yard thus cheerfully afforded scattered, natural egg nests. (At school weeks before Easter we planted grass seed in cottage cheese cartons and set them in the window to be sun-nurtured: Easter baskets awaiting coloring and pipe-cleaner handles.)

Formal, organized egg hunts were unknown to us and probably would not have been successful had some well-meaning adult suggested them. Instead, we preferred backyard searches where eggs were hidden in elm branches, on swing seats, under still-dry rustling shrubs, and on the Y-tongue of wagons. Our searches were honest and reliable, the hiders clever but never deceitful. We tried only to be imaginative in hiding eggs for the younger children, not confusing.

Two kinds of children lived in my neighborhood then: those who ate their colored, hard-boiled Easter eggs and those who didn't. Being of the latter group, I suspected those of the former to be vulgar and insensitive. After the careful time spent

in dyeing the eggs—such clean, solid, magical ellipses—they were cherished until their exteriors cracked and peeled to expose silky, yellowing film beneath, certainly inedible.

The dyeing process incorporated several hours of work. The eggs were delivered to our house by Mr. Bartel, whom we affectionately called "the egg man." Each Friday he picked up our two empty egg cartons and left two cartons full of fresh eggs, brown or white and—at least, I imagined—warm. As fresh as they were, the eggs were still good for boiling and dyeing. Mother set out the custard cups and into each one we put a tablet of color. It was, eye-watering vinegar and all, a labor of love.

Easter is also remembering several books I found so special. The large, slick green cover contained the story of the brown speckled egg and the unexpected friendship of a duck and a bunny, *The Golden Egg Book*. The last line comforted particu-larly: "And no one was ever alone again." The second book, *The Country Bunny and the Little Gold Shoes*, contained gentle pictures of a lovely, intricately painted sugar egg and the story of a brave, dutiful mother.

In Sunday school (where my mother or father seemed always to be my teacher) I enjoyed story time with the book which had typical 1950's illus-trations of a family, perfect and happy and blessed at Easter time. It was a book of prayers by Peter Marshall.

At church on Easter Sunday the warm air seemed fused with the heady fragrance of the lilies. On the piano was a bowl of early tulips, red and yellow and lavender. Hands stiff in unfamiliar white gloves and feet in stricture by unfamiliar black patent shoes, I sat in the pew and waited— happily and expectantly—for the miracle.

Cindy Hoffman

Easter Service

April washed the hillside;
Scrubbed clean each woodside lane;
And sprinkled on the meadows
Iris-scented rain.

Robins sang an anthem;
All Nature praised the King,
And placed before His altar
The offering of spring.

Barbara Yerbury Filan

Photo Opposite
"CON BRIO" IRIS
Michael Magnuson Photograph

A Call to Life and Hope

The voice of spring is gently soft
As bits of clouds on high,
A whispered message on the breeze
That gaily passes by.

'Tis echoed by the daffodil
And painted on the trees.
'Tis stamped upon each smiling face
For all the world to see.

It is a call to life and hope
With tasks that must be done,
A gentle harbinger of goals
That dreams are hinged upon.

It is a stirring call to faith
That vibrant spring imparts,
And certainly its message reigns
Within the human heart.

Craig Sathoff

Tulips

We tucked the bulbs within the earth
To wait till springtime gave them birth.

For five long months through winter snow,
We thought about the bulbs below,

Till March arrived, then up came spears,
Waving leaves like rabbit ears.

Then tall green stems began to rise
As raindrops fell out of the skies.

In April sun their cups unfolded,
Scarlet, pink, white and golden.

A heavenly beauty glows in each cup
As tulips lift their chalice up.

Ellen Martin

Photo Overleaf
WINDMILL AND TULIPS
Fred Sieb

Easter

Once more the Ancient Wonder
   Brings back the goose and crane
Prophetic Sons of Thunder,
   Apostles of the Rain.

In many a battling river
   The broken gorges boom.
Behold the Mighty Giver
   Emerges from the Tomb!

Now robins chant the story
   Of how the wintery sward
Is litten with the glory
   Of the Angel of the Lord.

His countenance is lightning,
　And still his robe is snow,
As when the dawn was brightening
　Two thousand years ago.

　O who can be a stranger
　　To what has come to pass?
　The Pity of the Manger
　　Is mighty in the grass!

　Undaunted by Decembers,
　　The sap is faithful yet,
　The giving Earth remembers
　　And only men forget!

　　　　　John G. Neihardt

Easter Came to Me

Easter enters every church,
She sits in every pew,
And flaunts her ribboned bonnet
Flowered with every hue.

Easter enters every church,
She walks down every aisle,
But I met her in the early dawn
In my newborn's smile.

I saw her when she gently passed
Through a meadow of pure jade,
And walked awhile with me beneath
The feathered plum tree's shade.

I watched her dance into the wind
Against pink-skirted orchard trees.
We listened to a meadow lark
In a sun-bright April breeze.

Easter came to church today,
But I met her in the field;
She wasn't half so prim and proud
Her own true self revealed.

Lucille Crumley

Sunrise Service

I shall worship in my garden
When the grass is wet with dew,
In a special sunrise service
When the Easter skies are blue.

There will be no massive pulpit
And no richly vested choir;
Just an altar built by nature
And a towering maple spire.

There will be no organ playing
With its loud and vibrant notes;
But a hymn of praise will echo
From a hundred songbird throats.

There I'll kneel in supplication
In a setting calm and still,
And sip lightly from the chalice
Of a golden daffodil.

Reginald Holmes

Symbol of Love

Easter comes in its own good time
And nature's beauty grows sublime.
We hear sweet echoes rise and swell
From silver tones of Easter bells.

And from the distance a lone bird's cry
And there against the sunset sky,
A cross outlined in stark relief
A symbol of love and true belief;
So near the cross is to a star
Like a benediction from afar.

With echoing bells upon the breeze
We bow in thanks for gifts like these.
All worthy gifts are highly priced
So bow and worship The Risen Christ.

Mamie Ozburn Odum

The Good Shepherd

I am the good shepherd,
and know my sheep, and am
known of mine.

As the Father knoweth
me, even so know I the
Father: and I lay down my
life for the sheep.

And other sheep I have,
which are not of this fold:
them also I must bring,
and they shall hear my
voice; and there shall be
one fold, and one shepherd.

John 10:14-16

Photo Opposite
THE GOOD SHEPHER
Gary Blodgett

I AM THE GOOD SHEPHERD. JOHN 10:11

The Triumphant Entry

And when he was come nigh, even now at the descent of the mount of Olives, the whole multitude of the disciples began to rejoice and praise God with a loud voice for all the mighty works that they had seen;

Saying, "Blessed be the King that cometh in the name of the Lord: peace in heaven, and glory in the highest."

And some of the Pharisees from among the multitude said unto him, "Master, rebuke thy disciples."

And he answered and said unto them, "I tell you that, if these should hold their peace, the stones would immediately cry out."

Luke 19:37-40

The Greatest Commandments

And one of the scribes came, and having heard them reasoning together, and perceiving that he had answered them well, asked him, "Which is the first commandment of all?"

And Jesus answered him, "The first of all the commandments is, Hear, O Israel; the Lord our God is one Lord:

"And thou shalt love the Lord thy God with all thy heart, and with all thy soul, and with all thy mind, and with all thy strength: this is the first commandment.

"And the second is like, namely this, Thou shalt love thy neighbour as thyself. There is no other commandment greater than these."

Mark 12:28-31

Photo Overleaf
THE TRIUMPHANT ENTRY
Three Lions

The Last Supper

Now the first day of the feast of unleavened bread the disciples came to Jesus, saying unto him, "Where wilt thou that we prepare for thee to eat the passover?"

And he said, "Go into the city to such a man, and say unto him, 'The Master saith, "My time is at hand; I will keep the passover at thy house with my disciples."

And the disciples did as Jesus had appointed them; and they made ready the passover.

Now when the even was come, he sat down with the twelve.

And as they did eat, he said, "Verily I say unto you, that one of you shall betray me."

And they were exceeding sorrowful, and began every one of them to say unto him, "Lord, is it I?"

And he answered and said, "He that dippeth his hand with me in the dish, the same shall betray me.

"The Son of man goeth as it is written of him: but woe unto that man by whom the Son of man is betrayed! it had been good for that man if he had not been born."

Then Judas, which betrayed him, answered and said, "Master, is it I?" He said unto him, "Thou hast said."

And as they were eating, Jesus took bread, and blessed it, and brake it, and gave it to the disciples, and said, "Take, eat; this is my body."

And he took the cup, and gave thanks, and gave it to them, saying, "Drink ye all of it;

"For this is my blood of the new testament, which is shed for many for the remission of sins.

"But I say unto you, I will not drink henceforth of this fruit of the vine, until that day when I drink it new with you in my Father's kingdom."

Matthew 26:17-29

The Crucifixion

Then came Jesus forth, wearing the crown of thorns, and the purple robe. And Pilate saith unto them, "Behold the man!"

When the chief priests therefore and officers saw him, they cried out, saying, "Crucify him, crucify him." Pilate saith unto them, "Take ye him, and crucify him: for I find no fault in him."

The Jews answered him, "We have a law, and by our law he ought to die, because he made himself the Son of God."

When Pilate therefore heard that saying, he was the more afraid;

And went again into the judgment hall, and saith unto Jesus, "Whence art thou?" But Jesus gave him no answer.

Then saith Pilate unto him, "Speakest thou not unto me? knowest thou not that I have power to crucify thee, and have power to release thee?"

Jesus answered, "Thou couldest have no power at all against me, except it were given thee from above: therefore he that delivered me unto thee hath the greater sin."

And from thenceforth Pilate sought to release him: but the Jews cried out, saying, "If thou let this man go, thou art not Caesar's friend: whosoever maketh himself a king speaketh against Caesar."

And it was the preparation of the passover, and about the sixth hour: and he saith unto the Jews, "Behold your King!"

But they cried out, "Away with him, away with him, crucify him, crucify him." Pilate saith unto them, "Shall I crucify your King?" The chief priests answered, "We have no king but Caesar."

Then delivered he him therefore unto them to be crucified. And they took Jesus and led him away.

And he bearing his cross went forth into a place called the place of a skull, which is called in the Hebrew Golgotha:

Where they crucified him, and two others with him, on either side one, and Jesus in the midst.

And Pilate wrote a title, and put it on the cross. And the writing was, JESUS OF NAZARETH, THE KING OF THE JEWS.

John 19:5-19

The Resurrection

Now upon the first day of the week, very early in the morning, they came unto the sepulchre, bringing the spices which they had prepared, and certain others with them.

And they found the stone rolled away from the sepulchre.

And they entered in, and found not the body of the Lord Jesus.

And it came to pass, as they were much perplexed thereabout, behold, two men stood by them in shining garments:

And as they were afraid, and bowed down their faces to the earth, they said unto them, "Why seek ye the living among the dead?

"He is not here, but is risen: remember how he spake unto you when he was yet in Galilee,

"Saying, 'The Son of man must be delivered into the hands of sinful men, and be crucified, and the third day rise again.'"

And they remembered his words,

And returned from the sepulchre, and told all these things unto the eleven, and to all the rest.

It was Mary Magdalene, and Joanna, and Mary the mother of James, and other women that were with them, which told these things unto the apostles.

And their words seemed to them as idle tales, and they believed them not.

Then arose Peter, and ran unto the sepulchre; and stooping down, he beheld the linen clothes laid by themselves, and departed, wondering in himself at that which was come to pass.

Luke 24: 1-12

The Other Woman at the Tomb

The morning was dark and damp as the women scurried along silently through the sleeping streets. Judith clutched the bundle of aromatic spices tightly, the scent of myrrh winding about her like a funeral shroud. She shuddered. She didn't want to be here, not like this. As the pale fingers of the dawn crept along the distant hill, the birds began to call to each other. To Judith they sounded like cries of warning. Her heart pounded. Her lungs ached. Her head throbbed.

"Hurry," Mary of Magdala called over her shoulder.

"But what if there are soldiers?" the other Mary cried in a gasping whisper. "And what about the stone?"

Judith's mind raced backwards even as her feet swept across the dewy weeds. How could it have come to this? Only weeks ago she had followed the Master, drinking in his words like a parched desert drinks in water. Ever since his touch had healed her, she had trailed after him, hauling cool water, bringing bread and barley cakes, running errands for the disciples. Once destitute and empty, her life finally had meaning and purpose. Only seven days ago, in the streets of Jerusalem, she had seen her master hailed as king. Even now, the memory brought a thrill of joy. But as suddenly as thunderclouds on a summer day, events had tumbled and crashed about her. The Master was arrested, tried, mocked, crucified, buried and it was all over. Ended. Hope was as dead as the body they had carried from the cross.

Tears traced their familiar paths down Judith's cheeks. How could Mary do it? What kept her determination fired? This was foolish. They could all be killed. Suddenly, Mary stopped and Judith nearly fell against her. The small group of women stood panting in the velvety shadows of a huge acacia.

"Look!" Judith's whisper rang with awe.

The women stared. Ahead of them, like a gaping black wound, stood the open tomb. The heavy stone, intended to seal the crypt, was pushed aside. There were no guards, no soldiers, no sounds but the sighing breezes and the crying birds.

Mary Magdalene walked slowly forward toward the opening, never taking her eyes from the blackness within. Judith felt drawn, almost against her will, to follow. She reached to grasp the other Mary's hand—as cold and clammy as her own—and together they edged toward the tomb.

Judith wanted to run away; away from the dark, cold, death-drenched place, back to the city where life throbbed with color and sound. But she stayed, compelled by something stronger than herself.

Slowly, the women entered the cool dimness of the tomb. Once inside they stood paralyzed with wonder, filled with fear.

"Don't be frightened." The voice was deep and resonant, full of strength, yet tempered with kindness. Light radiated from the speaker, a young man robed in dazzling white.

Judith stared at the earthen floor of the tomb, fearful of meeting the piercing gaze of the speaker.

"Why do you seek the living among the dead?" he asked. "Don't you recall Jesus said he would rise again from the dead?"

The two questions rang in Judith's ears and echoed in her heart. She dared a glance at the unearthly stranger and his eyes caught hers and held them.

"Go now and tell the others. He is risen. You shall see him again."

Judith's heart pounded. Alive? The Master was alive!

Mary Magdalene's urgency cut through Judith's awe. "Come! Come quickly!"

The others were already outside, dashing like children down the dawn-pink road. Judith turned once more to the tomb. The stranger was gone. The light had faded. The tomb was dark.

But in her heart, she had captured the brilliance of the words "He is risen." The death knell was silenced, the night of grief was past and, in the freshness of the shining dawn, Judith discovered the truth at last. The tomb was not the end of it all. It was only the beginning.

Pamela Kennedy

The Miracle of Easter

All Nature cried that dark, drear day
When Christ hung on the cross,
While darkness filled the heavens above
Earth trembled at the loss.

The sad disciples' hearts were wrung
With grief for all to see,
They saw no hope, for lo, their Lord
Had died on Calvary.

But hope and life came with the dawn
Of glorious Easter Day,
"The Lord is risen," were the words
The lilies seemed to say.

All Nature thrilled and cried in tune
"A victory is won.
Our Lord has risen from the dead
New life has now begun."

Carice Williams

Alone

The ones who'd followed drew
    away
The night the Master knelt
    to pray
    Beside the garden stone.
The three their vigil couldn't
    keep.
Instead they dozed and fell
    asleep
    And left Him quite alone.

No others shared His thoughts
    that night
For they possessed restricted
    sight.
     They saw a mortal throne.
The cup His prayer could
    not remove
Time, too, He knew was sure
    to prove
     As His and His alone.

By Peter thrice He was
    denied.
The one He'd cherished left
    and lied
     About the man they'd known.
On His behalf none spoke a
    word
To Him it must have oft
    occurred
     How much He was alone.

Margaret Rorke

Daffodils

Spring has a way of painting
  The meadow with delight,
With all the crowning glory
  Of the daffodils so bright!

For beams of yellow sunshine
  From a watercolor sky
Seem to cast their glow of magic
  All along the countryside.

Until there comes the moment
  When the brilliancy is spun,
And the flowers meek and golden
  Lift their faces to the sun.

Then is the day exultant
  Where all of April smiles.
My joy is wrapped in wonder,
  And my way is dream-beguiled.

Joy Belle Burgess

Photo Opposite
WOODLAND DAFFODIL
Milton Baroody
Cyr Color

Viney Wilder Endicott

Viney Endicott was born in Philadelphia, Pennsylvania, and educated in Trenton, New Jersey. Her work has been featured in several anthologies and in magazines such as the *Saturday Evening Post*. Her poetry has also appeared in a variety of newspapers, including the *New York Times* and the *Christian Science Monitor*, and she regularly sells verses to greeting card companies. A student of dramatic as well as literary pursuits, Mrs. Endicott enjoys reading, teaching, and spending time with her family. She lives in the picturesque town of Cape May Court House, New Jersey.

March

March is bold, I do declare,
Taking folks so unaware,
Whisking hats from off the head,
Tearing news before it's read...

Chasing anything in sight,
Whistling at the doors all night,
Tossing ladies' hats awry,
Snapping clotheslines on the sly...

Howling in the wildest glee,
Stripping branches off a tree,
Just a scamp from end to end
Yet the children call him friend.

He it is who lifts their kites
Far above the chimney sights,
Joining in their boisterous fun,
Playing tag with everyone.

He is just a child at heart,
Playing tricks and being smart.
Let's forgive him since we know
April soon will steal his show.

Ideals to Live By

If we would live, not merely drift,
We must have ideals that will lift
Our eyes above the staid routine
To "see" with faith those things unseen.

To vision that integrity
That walks with men most truly free;
To ever heed the still small voice
Above the crowd's demanding choice.

Good teaching therefore will unite
Ideals and learning, bind them tight,
That growth of the true nobility
Shall keep the mind and spirit free
To build in every neighborhood
A common ground of brotherhood.

April Rain

The wild sweet rain of April spills
On golden-throated daffodils,
On garden wall and new green bough,
On earth fresh-turned before the plough.

It scrubs the pansy's small shy face
And shines each blade of grass in place
To leave the springtime world aglow,
And lift my heart to walk tiptoe.

Invasion

An army came invading
Our little town today,
And we were caught so unaware
Resistance went astray.

They did not come in tanks and jeeps,
They never made a sound,
Yet in they marched, triumphantly,
Backed by the underground.

Their camouflage removed, they stood
Erect in every yard
While we, their prisoners smiled to see
The daffodils on guard!

Reverie

Here in a meadow by the sea,
Summer is caught and held for me
In mounds of sun-drenched seasoned hay,
In yellow buttercups that play
The host to traveled honey bees
Alighting from the latest breeze;
In cricket's noonday serenade,
In ancient oak's refreshing shade,
In clover bloom and sunset's glow
Summer is here, in cameo.

Time

It cannot be bought and it cannot be sold,
It cannot be hoarded like silver and gold.
Yet they who have need of material things
May squander or use it as wisely as kings.

For God in His goodness has given us time
That we might invest it in Man's upward climb.
Of course, in the giving He won't specify
Just how we must use it as years hurry by.

He gives us a choice and a new chance each day
To value our minutes or toss them away,
But one thing is certain, whichever we choose,
We'll learn very soon Time has wings on his shoes!
And those who are wise will keep pace with each day
By learning to live in the noblest way.

Peter's Hideaway

In the land of the green meadows,
   Near a laughing little brook,
At the forest edge or orchard,
   There's a secret little nook.
Where Peter Rabbit hides away
   When troubles get him down
But soon he's peeking out again
   And hopping all around.

He scampers through the pasture
   And through the briar patch,
Encompassed with adventures
   And food that he can catch.
And oft' he visits Reddy Fox
   And Jerry Muskrat, too;
Jimmy Skunk and Turtle Dove
   Make up but just a few.

His friends are all the happy ones
   That make his life worthwhile.
And don't you think that Peter, too,
   Is loved by every child.

                  Edith M. Helstern

Dawn

I love the dawn, the gentle light of morning,
 When diamonds of the sky grow dim
 And golden Sun sneaks o'er the brim,
The newborn day adorning.

The little bunny, feeding in the bushes,
 Now scurries far away to hide
 Amid the rocks, and there abide
Far from the sun's bright blushes.

As dawn shall break, the songbird's joyful singing
 Blends with the beauty of the light
 To start another day just right,
A new hope always bringing.

Another day, thank God for glorious dawn,
 Which fades the darkness of the night
 And gives new faith and clearer sight—
That our hearts may carry on.

W. Earlington Whitney

Contentment

Green meadows stretch before me
With flowers here and there.
I see the yellow buttercups
And daisies everywhere.

Little sparrows on the wing
Are playful in the breeze.
The songs that they are singing
Are cheerful little glees!

Children are running through the grass;
I hear the rushing of a brook.
There are scenes of quiet beauty
Everywhere I look.

I think I'll stay forever here;
I've not desire to roam.
Why, this is just the perfect place
To make a happy home.

Patricia Joyce Keffer

Photo Overleaf
SPRING WILDFLOWERS
Jeff Gnass

A Modern Garden of Eden

Mary Lapham Hunt's eighteen-acre biblical garden in Ojai, California, is not only authentic and a visual delight, but also replete with surprises—some a little unsettling. For instance, did you know that Eve's legendary apple turns out to have been an *apricot*? That Solomon's rose of Sharon was actually a tiny tulip? That the manna from heaven that fed the children of Israel was not unleavened bread, but the hardened nutritious sap of the tall manna tree? What, baby Moses wasn't found in the bulrushes? No, the basket in which his sister placed him was made of bulrush.

Mary Hunt's biblical garden is indeed one continuing revelation.

It all began when she was looking for a unique display idea for her garden club's annual show. Inspiration struck as she stared at her pretty garden dotted with herbs and plants tracing their lineage to faraway Israel. Why not a miniature biblical garden as her contribution? "It was a pretty modest little exhibit," Mary confesses, "and I never dreamed it would get much attention, surrounded as it was by much more elegant arrangements. So you can imagine my surprise when it turned out to be a show-stopper."

A short time later, the minister of the Ojai Presbyterian Church offered her the eighteen acres adjoining his church's property if she would consent to reproduce her biblical garden on a larger scale—1800 square feet, to be exact. The planting and care of this modern garden of Eden would be completely under her supervision. It was an exciting challenge. "Well, why not?" she reasoned. "The Ojai climate is almost identical to the Holy Land's, so if I can locate the plants and herbs mentioned in the Scriptures, I can surely grow them."

There followed months of intensive research and regular consultations by mail with Dr. Harold M. Modenke, curator of the New York Botanical Garden and the world's foremost biblical botanist. Gradually, Mary Hunt turned barren land into a spectacular garden boasting over 200 authentic specimens. "Actually, there are more [specimens] here than can be found in Israel today," she says during her conducted tour. (She now has five docents assisting in these wondrous walks through biblical history.)

The mood is set at the very beginning by a huge sundial, which is a duplicate of those used by biblical prophets. Nearby, a proud Cedar of Lebanon reminds visitors of Ezekiel's words to Egypt's Pharoah: "To what shall I compare you in your greatness? Surely to a Cedar of Lebanon."

Nearby, a lovely spreading palm almost brushes the cedar's giant branches. "I call that palm my gift from heaven—literally," says Mary. Chuckling, she

gives an account of her long search for an authentic biblical palm. "Yes, I know we have desert palms here in California, but they're hybrids and I was determined to find the identical one so often mentioned in the Scriptures. Well, numerous dedicated botanists joined in my quest—as they did for many of my other specimens. Then, out of the blue, I received a letter from Mr. D.L. Heaven—truly, that is his name—saying he had a palm tree such as I was looking for, and he'd donate it to my garden if I'd transport it from his home in Palm Springs. I checked it out and—lo and behold—it *was* the palm I was looking for!" It took that determined lady a year before she was able to bring the tree to her Ojai garden.

In biblical times, plants were cultivated for food, shade or medicinal purposes. Their beauty was incidental. Take the herb known as *rue*. It was so generally used in food preparation, as well as believed to have the power to ward off plagues, that it served as an acceptable tithe in place of shekels. Luke 11:42 states, "For ye tithe mint and rue and all manner of herbs."

Sharing a spot with the oft-mentioned nettles of yore is a shower of pretty little white blossoms with the unsightly name "Dove's dung." The flower springs from a tiny poisonous bulb, Mary explained, but it was considered a delicacy when the poison was carefully boiled out.

Another bright spot is a patch of myrtle with its shining blue-green leaves and fragrant white blossoms. Because it is symbolic of happiness and joy, brides of Europe traditionally include a spray in their wedding bouquets or hair. Even Princess Diana insisted that her lavish wedding bouquet contain a bit of myrtle.

A peek into the garden's guest book reveals that visitors have come from far and wide to view this unique horticultural display. One recent visitor, Baron Alfred Rothschild of Italy, remarked that he had seen nothing like it in Europe. Another man, after learning about Eve's apple, laughingly remarked, "Now I'll have to call my wife the 'apricot of my eye'!"

Scattered among the garden's biblical plants are authentic artifacts contributed by visitors as appropriate memorials. Others have included remembrances in their wills. Since the biblical garden is completely self-supporting, Mary Hunt acknowledges that such gifts are most welcome. A modest fee is charged for a conducted tour or visitors may roam on their own for free.

Each plant in the garden is identified with a bronze plaque listing the common and biblical nomenclature and the biblical verse where the plant is mentioned. Visitors to the garden may join a conducted tour or they may roam on their own, enjoying the solace and inspiration of Mary Hunt's living biblical history.

Margaret Cool

Season of Promise

The crab apple has budded and blossomed;
Its petals are pink in the lane.
The grasses are green on the hillsides,
And lilacs are sweet in the rain.

The earth has been furrowed and planted,
And the seed thrusts up spear after spear.
This is the season of promise;
This is the spring of the year.

Edith Shaw Butler

Spring Comes Every Year

Spring came to the valley
At sunup today,
And melted the snows in
An artistic way.
It lifted the leaves from
Each shell-covered bud
And smiled when it saw the
Narcissi in nod.

Spring came to the valley
When dawn filled the sky
And opened the eyelid of
Each sleeping eye.
It tinted the grass with
Chlorophyll green
And warmly embraced the
Ice-covered stream.

Spring came to the valley,
It comes every year;
If we will but harken,
Its message we'll hear:
The winter is past,
Rejoice all and sing:
The earth is alive with
The coming of spring.

Loise Pinkerton Fritz

A Tribute to Mothers

Our next issue, Mother's Day Ideals, celebrates the various stages of motherhood—from the new mother's first thoughts of her child to the nostalgic remembrances of "like Mother used to make."

Join us as we share the Mother's Day memories of Al Capp, Lansing Christman, Margaret Rorke, and some of our loyal readers in a colorful tribute to mothers everywhere. You can also share the joy with a friend by sending a gift subscription, starting with Mother's Day Ideals.

ACKNOWLEDGEMENTS

IT'S ALMOST SPRING, LORD from *Bubble Gum & Chalk Dust* by Mary Lou Carney. Copyright© 1982 by Abingdon Press. Used by permission; EASTER from *Lyric and Dramatic Poems*, copyright by John G. Neihardt, published by the University of Nebraska Press. Permission granted by The John G. Neihardt Trust. Our sincere thanks to the following people whose addresses we were unable to locate: Frances Bowles for FINDING EASTER EGGS; Beatrice Branch for EASTER; Joy Belle Burgess for DAFFODILS; Leila Bishopp Martin for EASTER PROMISE; and W. Earlington Whitney for DAWN from *Reveries of the Old Homesteader*, copyright© 1946 by W. Earlington Whitney.